TOULOUSE-LAUTREC

MARIA CIONINI VISANI

GROSSET & DUNLAP
Publishers - New York

First American edition published by Grosset & Dunlap, Inc.
All rights reserved
Translated from the Italian by Pearl Sanders
Translation copyright © 1971 by Thames and Hudson, London
Copyright © 1969 by Sadea Editore, Firenze
Library of Congress Catalog Card Number: 75-122026

Printed and bound in Italy

Life

The two factors in the life of Henri-Marie-Raymond de Toulouse-Lautrec Monfa which can never be ignored are his noble birth and the tragedy of his misshapen body. These two essential factors, and especially the latter, determined the course of his life and also provided a rich field for the romantic imagination of some of his biographers. Yet however much we may wish to avoid such a romanticized view of his life, we cannot act as if these things did not exist, and all we can do is to ensure that their importance is not exaggerated.

Toulouse-Lautrec was born at Albi in the night of 24 November 1864. His parents were first cousins, Count Alphonse de Toulouse-Lautrec Monfa and Adèle Tapié de Céleyran, whose titles of nobility can be traced to the time of Charlemagne. Their ancestors were warriors and lords of Languedoc and Provence; Raymond VI, Count of Toulouse, was the defender of the Albigensian Catharists and was defeated by Innocent III in 1229; and Odet de Foix, Viscount of Lautrec, was made governor of the Milan province by Francis I as a reward for his valour at the Battle of Marignan. In less heroic times, the family was one of the most highly esteemed in the South of France, and continued the aristocratic tradition of riding and hunting. Count Alphonse does not seem to have been without good qualities, and in his individualism, his vivacity and his impatience of constraint he was close to his son.

When Henri was born, his father presented him with a book on falconry, in which he wrote these words: ' Remember, my son, that an open-air life is the only healthy life there is: everything which is deprived of liberty withers and dies in a short space of time. This little book on falconry will teach you how to enjoy the life of the open countryside, and if one day you come to know the sorrows of life, then the horse first, and after the horse the dog and falcon, will be your dear companions and will enable you to forget your sorrows '.

But when, only too soon, fate struck its blow, the heir to this long tradition was unable to thrust his despair on to either the horse or the falcon, however much he had come to love them in the first happy years of his childhood, which were spent in the country at his mother's châteaux of Bosc and Céleyran. Henri's father felt himself betrayed by his deformed son, who could never hope to be part of the elegant outdoor life which was his birthright, and to a large extent he lost interest in him. When some years later a friend wrote discreetly to tell the Count of the serious condition of his son's life, his reply was to advise him to go to live in England, where ' drunkards pass unnoticed '. Only on his deathbed did the Count show some signs of remorse.

Fortunately, Henri's mother did understand him. If his father passed on to him his love of shocking an audience and his brilliant imagination, his mother gave him her most tender love and her constant support, and chose to overlook the irregularity of a life which differed so greatly from her own. A disappointed wife and a cruelly afflicted mother (a second son, Richard, died when he was only a few months old), she bore her unhappiness with the same courage with which her son met his infirmity.

But in the early years of Henri's life there was no indication of the cruel fate which was in store for him. He grew up as a happy and lively child in the company of numerous cousins, learned to ride and received his first lessons in Latin and Greek. In 1872 he moved with his family to Paris and became a pupil of the Lycée Fontanes, where he met Maurice Joyant, who was to become his lifelong friend, author of a basic study of the artist and the founder of the Musée Toulouse-Lautrec at Albi. Toulouse-Lautrec was a modest pupil, and was popular with his friends, whom he amused by filling his exercise books and the margins of text books with caricatures of teachers and fellow-pupils and with animal sketches. But his mother became worried about his health and withdrew him from school; in 1874 she took him back to Albi, where he continued his studies with a private tutor. He also spent some time at the spa of Amélie-les-Bains, again because his physical development was causing anxiety.

On 30 May 1878, in the drawing-room of the château at Albi, he stumbled and fell, breaking his left thigh; his leg was put into plaster, and he spent a long time convalescing at Barèges, near Amélie-les-Bains. Fourteen months later, while walking with his mother near Barèges, he fell into the dry bed of a stream and fractured his right thigh. The tragedy was now complete: his fragile bones did not heal and his body remained stunted (for generations the Toulouse-Lautrec and Tapié de Céleyran families had intermarried, and it is probable that this was the remote cause of the child's bone deficiency). Retrospective diagnosis, which is of course very difficult, would seem to indicate that he suffered from Clément's polyepiphysary dystrophy, a disease in which the bony tissue around the epiphysis becomes brittle. The two fractures were therefore ' pathological ', that is to say, they were a consequence of the state of his bones.

The next three years were spent at Albi, Nice (in winter), Céleyran, and the spas of Barèges and Amélie-les-Bains; in the long, melancholy years of suffering and ' cures ', Lautrec evinced remarkable fortitude. With the encouragement of his parents and friends, he immersed himself in his drawings, making rapid sketches of everything he saw and through this activity finding some forgetfulness and pleasure. He also continued his studies and obtained his *baccalauréat* in November 1881, after an unsuccessful attempt in July. In the same year he made twenty-three drawings to illustrate *Cocotte*, a short story by his friend Etienne Devismes. From then on he devoted himself entirely to drawing, which allowed him to live a more intense and exciting inner life to compensate for the active life he was forced to renounce. It seems that by rapidly putting down on paper the movements of horses and birds he found some consolation for his deformed physique and the enforced immobility which was fate's answer to his youthful eagerness for life.

In March 1882 his mother, who always encouraged him,

let him go to Paris to work in the studio of René Princeteau, an animal painter from Bordeaux and a friend of Count Alphonse, who admired and encouraged him. Later, when Princeteau saw that he could not teach his pupil adequately, he introduced him to Léon Bonnat, a successful but boring and derivative artist. Lautrec was a diligent pupil and worked hard to master his art; in his eagerness to learn, he accepted the historical and mythological themes, the dark colours and magniloquent gestures taught by his master. Bonnat's response to his pupil's efforts was not very encouraging: ' Your painting's not bad, it has some elegance; no, it's not bad, but your drawing is simply atrocious '. But three months later Bonnat's studio closed; Lautrec, together with some of the other pupils, moved to the studio of Fernand Cormon at 10 Rue Constance, on the slopes of Montmartre. Here the atmosphere was warmer and happier than at Bonnat's. Although Cormon was an enthusiast about history and antiquity (his academic painting *Cain* was exhibited at the 1880 Salon), he was a jovial man and was tolerant towards the new trends.

In Cormon's studio Lautrec met Anquetin, Gauzi, Bernard and Grenier, the first of a large circle of friends, who saw in the witty, courteous ' *petit homme* ' the unsurpassable instigator of pranks and entertainments. While Lautrec's studio drawings show the influence of the academic style of Cormon, his drawings of horses and men, which were created spontaneously, free from the constraint of studio lessons, and also the portraits drawn in the hospitable garden of Père Forest, reveal a draughtsmanship which already contained a highly personal note — in spite of a certain affinity with Impressionism.

It was in the garden of Père Forest that he painted the *Portrait of Marie* (Buenos Aires, Museo Nacional de Bellas Artes); the sitter was Suzanne Valadon, the mother of Maurice Utrillo, a cynical and elusive woman who represented one of the most bitter of Lautrec's emotional experiences.

In art, Lautrec found a reason for living, as he did in his circle of lively and fun-loving friends, who were always eager to respond to the stimuli of novelty and eccentricity. In 1884 he left Cormon's studio and went to live at the house of Grenier, whose beautiful wife Lily had sat for Degas when he lived in the same house; all Lautrec's biographers record his emotion when some years later, in 1893, Degas was moved to exclaim before one of his paintings: '*Çà, Lautrec, on voit que vous êtes du bâtiment*'. (Well, Lautrec, one can see you belong to the house).

In 1885, Lautrec met Van Gogh in Cormon's studio. In connection with this meeting it would be interesting to be able to speak of reciprocal influences, but there is no real basis for such an assumption, even though at this period Lautrec was painting in a way not unlike that of the Dutchman (for example, in the portraits of Van Gogh and Justine Dieuhl), and later it was Lautrec who suggested to Van Gogh in 1888 that he should go to Provence to find the sun he needed for his health and the light which was vital to his painting. Any similarity between them must rather be put down to an affinity in their natures and temperaments. Both artists belong to the period of post-impressionism, when drawing was considered as the necessary support for pictorial expression, and line was used as a means of subtly penetrating the essence of objects and characters by denuding them of their covering of flesh, rather than as a means of decoration. Also, as a result of their unhappy experiences, both artists had come to achieve a conscious mixture of art and life — one of them in grim despair, the other with ironical detachment.

A determining factor in Lautrec's artistic development was his friendship with Aristide Bruant. Bruant was a composer and performer of songs and the editor of a magazine, *Le Mirliton*; Lautrec was fascinated by his anarchism, his sudden bursts of ingenuous affection, and his show of culture coloured by verbal vulgarity. Bruant was without doubt a snob, but the kind of snob Lautrec liked. Some of his best posters were made for Bruant, and he made many drawings and vignettes for *Le Mirliton*. Bruant reciprocated the artist's admiration and warm friendship (he agreed to sing solo at the opening of the cabaret Les

Ambassadeurs only on condition that the poster was by Lautrec). Through his collaboration with the singer, Lautrec came into contact with the bohemian underworld, with all its squalor and its animal vitality. In 1884, Lautrec set up a studio in the Rue Tourlaque; at that time he was living with Henri Rachou. In 1887-93 he lived with his friend Dr Bourges, not far away in Rue Fontaine.

This was the heart of Montmartre, still a strange village at the edge of Paris. In front of Lautrec's studio stretched the *maquis*, a conglomeration of low huts standing among green fields and lilac bushes; chicken and rabbit-runs leaned against their walls. It was rare for the good citizens of Paris to venture so far: although in the daytime the farmyard animals and the smell of hay gave the *maquis* an innocent rural air, at night the dark streets were the headquarters of robbers and murderers who came there to settle their accounts — unless they were disturbed by the sudden incursions of the police. The same darkness sheltered the street walkers and gave them some protection from the brutality of their men. But literary fashion and a growing interest in the social life of the underworld encouraged artists to seek their inspiration among these night dwellers. And when Montmartre became a centre of amusement, with cabarets, bars, theatres and brothels springing up everywhere, the curiosity of many middle-class citizens was aroused; they came to find in the under-world the sensations denied them in their daily lives, when they had to act the part of righteous, self-satisfied and respectable citizens, the severe custodians of family morality.

These were the most fertile years of Lautrec's artistic production, when he found his source of inspiration in the streets and bars; it is easy to see a connection between this subject matter and that of all the ' social ' literature of the period, whose most significant representative was Emile Zola. But Lautrec was not a cultured man, in our sense of the word: he hardly ever read a book, and his education was very imperfect. We can therefore merely say that Lautrec necessarily reflected the climate in which he lived, and if at first we may be tempted to see in him the 'Maupassant of painting' (Filippo de Pisis, 1931), we can only reject this view when we compare the detachment of the writer with the excitement and intensity of the painter. In this Lautrec represents something new, since he is not afraid to 'compromise' himself emotionally: before him Constantin Guys had also portrayed girls on the street and in brothels, but he had seen them as pretty, flirtatious creatures, whereas the dull faces of Lautrec's girls are without the saving grace of charm and express a tragic sorrow.

'Like a familiar and benevolent gnome', wrote Pierre Mac Orlan, 'he reigned over the poorly lighted streets of Montmartre, where shadows play an important role. His kingdom stretched from Place Pigalle to Place Clichy'; and Maurice Joyant tells how at the Moulin Rouge, 'always seated at the same place so as to have the same view, he had become a legendary figure'. Besides the Moulin Rouge, Lautrec assiduously frequented the Café du Rat-Mort, the Bal du Moulin de la Galette, Bruant's Le Mirliton, Le Chat Noir, Le Divan Japonais and the Bal de l'Elysée Montmartre. He was already drinking heavily, but drew unceasingly, the rapid line of his pencil noting down a profile, a hand, the fleeting motion of a foot raised in dancing, a mouth in a grimace of joy or disgust, satiety or anxiety. Later, in the calm of his studio he worked slowly on these sketches and out of them were born La Goulue and Valentin, Bruant, Yvette Guilbert, Jane Avril, Loïe Fuller, Marcelle Lender, all the stars of Montmartre whose ephemeral glory was immortalized by his hand.

Large numbers of photographs (for this cripple not only had no fear of being photographed in all kinds of moods and poses, but actually signed his invitations and menus with a light sketch of his own maimed silhouette) reveal him to us as the familiar figure he had become to the inhabitants of Montmartre: black and white checked trousers, bowler, blue cape and a green scarf tied round his neck. He was extremely ugly, and the merciless description of Yvette Guilbert is probably not so very exaggerated: 'Picture the large head of Gnafron [a grotesque puppet] on the body of a dwarf. An enormous dark head, a highly-coloured face, a black beard; greasy, oily skin; a nose which would be sufficient for two faces; and a mouth . . . ah, it was a mouth like a rag, a mouth resembling a wound. The lips were tumid and purplish, and closed flabbily over the timorous, soft and humid fissure of the mouth '.

However, the photographs sometimes also reveal, behind the lenses of the *pince-nez*, eyes which, if not enough to compensate for his physical ugliness, at least provide an answer — were the works not enough! — to those who judged him to be an evil genius or vindictive monster: they were deep black eyes, which evoked the happiness of which he had been deprived by fate, an ancient sorrow, a nostalgia which his lucid awareness of reality told him could never be placated. He must have had a sense of sin, but it was the consciousness of a sad fatality, which he accepted but did not judge; in fact, he immersed himself in it and yielded to the violence of his native sensuality; as he pitilessly wore out his body, he sought to forget the healthy, robust man imprisoned in the figure of an eccentric dwarf.

From 1891 onwards, Lautrec spent short periods in the brothels of the Rue des Moulins and Rue d'Amboise — as Van Gogh, Bernard and Raffaëlli had done before him. These visits inspired an album of drawings, *Elles*, published in 1896, and the decoration of the drawing-room of the Rue d'Amboise brothel with sixteen medallions — now dispersed. The album *Elles*, where the prostitutes were portrayed in all sincerity and without any idealization, aroused considerable antagonism among the solid citizens, who had once accused Baudelaire of the same subversion of morality. Yet there is nothing sensual about the way these women are depicted. The artist lived among them as their friend, shared their meals and listened to their confidences, and he found in them the qualities and defects which are common to every human existence. It was the naturalness of his approach which enabled him to uncover the naïve simplicity of his subjects; out of the respect and pity he felt for his sad heroines there emerged the moral lesson of a man who throughout his life repudiated any kind of moralizing. What had once happened to Flaubert now befell Lautrec as well: the teaching contained in the work of art came into existence against the will of the artist, as if to spite his convictions and stated beliefs. These women had the added advantage of being ideal models because they could move about naked without embarrassment, and since Lautrec lived among them, he could seize any moment to capture them in a natural and intimate pose. He used to say, ' *Le modèle est toujours empaillé; elles, elles vivent* ' (the model is always a stuffed dummy, but *they* are alive).

In February 1893 Lautrec held his first exhibition together with Charles Maurin — a fashionable cartoonist — at the Boussod et Valadon Gallery: critics (Gustave Geffroy in *La Justice*, Roger Marx in *La Rapide*) praised his psychological insight, his ferocious wit, and his originality as an artist who was indifferent to rules and systems. Success was not new to Lautrec: his work had been well received in 1888 when he showed eleven works at the Exposition des Vingt held in Brussels, which was then the centre for new art trends; from 1889 to 1894 he participated regularly each year in the exhibitions of the Paris Salon des Indépendants; in 1890 and 1892 he again sent in work to Brussels and in 1892 won considerable acclaim in Paris at the Cercle Volnay and the Galerie Le Barc de Boutteville.

In 1894 he accompanied Joyant to London, where he met Oscar Wilde; it is well known that Lautrec was an anglophile, in common with all the snobbish intellectual society of Paris, and it is not surpising that he enjoyed the company of the aesthetes, whose standard-bearers were Wilde and Whistler. He must have greatly enjoyed Wilde's wit and originality of thought, as well as Whistler's ' nocturnes ' and Japanese fantasies; we know also how greatly he admired the cerebral decorative art of Beardsley — in that he was probably alone among Parisians. The admiration must have been mutual, since Whistler gave a banquet in his honour at the Savoy, and Beardsley, whose first initiation to hashish occurred in the studio of Lautrec, sent him a copy of his *Book of Fifty Drawings* as a mark of esteem. England was the only foreign country Lautrec liked; he was not a traveller, for he was not one of those who seek through travel a means of escape; neither was he thrilled by the excitement of setting out on a journey. He was not even moved by an overwhelming curiosity; he rarely visited museums, though he waxed enthusiastic over Cranach's *Man in Red* when he saw it in Brussels, and the paintings of Velázquez and Uccello in the National Gallery in London; from Spain, with the exception of Goya and El Greco, he returned disappointed. Instead of travel he preferred to spend his summers with his friends, or at Valvins in the carefree company of Thadée Natanson, the editor of the *Revue blanche*, and his beautiful wife Misia; there he enjoyed easy-going conversation and the music of Misia, whom he asked a hundred times to repeat Beethoven's *Ruins of Athens*. Sometimes he went sailing and swimming at Arcachon and Toussot, or returned home to Malromé and Celeyran, where his mother, the only person whose pity he was able to accept, awaited him.

In May 1897 he left Rue Tourlaque and moved to 5 Avenue Franchot. He continued to work, but now his interest centred on the world of sport, the Comédie Française and the Opéra; when his cousin Gabriel Tapié de Céleyran came to Paris, he became interested in the world of medicine also (he drew the famous surgeon Péan while he was operating at Saint-Louis hospital); the law courts, too, provided inspiration.

He was now an alcoholic, worn and old before his time, and had already advanced far along the path which in March 1899 was to lead him to the clinic of Dr Sémelaigne at 16 Avenue de Madrid, Neuilly, suffering from hallucinations, amnesia and *delirium tremens*. Once alcohol was denied him, he soon recovered, and executed thirty-nine drawings of circus life without the aid of notes or sketches. These drawings provided proof that he had recovered his sanity, and the doctors let him go but declared that it was vital to keep a constant watch over him. Lautrec accepted the surveillance of a distant relative, Paul Viaud: this pleasant companion was also a good sailor, and together they made frequent journeys to Normandy, Le Crotoy, Le

Havre, Bordeaux, Arcachon and Toussot, and again to Malromé.

When Lautrec returned to Paris in the autumn of 1899 he found that his prices had risen considerably after the publicity aroused by his stay at Neuilly. He began to paint again: the powerful portrait of *Madame Poupoule*, the tender *Croquesi-Margouin (pls 76-77)*, *Maurice Joyant (pl. 75)* and *Viaud dressed as an English eighteenth-century admiral*, as well as the drawings for the production of *La Belle Hélène* at Bordeaux *(pl. 74)*, where he spent the winter, give proof of an unconquered energy, a love of life so intense that it brought him to his death. When he left Paris on 15 July 1901, neither his friends nor he himself were deceived: this is proved by the fact that before he left he took care to complete the unfinished works, to sign paintings and drawings and to put his studio in good order. On 15 August he was struck by paralysis and asked to be taken to Malromé. Here he still managed to paint; exhausted, almost unable to touch food, his poor legs stiffened by paralysis, he was lifted on to a ladder and worked feverishly to complete his great *Portrait of Viaud* and *Examination at the Faculty of Medicine (pls 78-79)*. Only a few days remained: on 9 September at 2.15 a.m., the last heir to the nobility of Provence and the Albigensian rebellion died in his mother's arms. He was buried at Saint-André-du-Bois, but later the Countess feared that a proposed road development might disturb the peace of the cemetery and had his body removed to Verdelais (Gironde).

Works

When Toulouse-Lautrec first arrived in Paris in 1882 at the age of sixteen, the great period of Impressionism was at its end: the 1886 exhibition was the last one held by the group, and of its original members only Degas and Pissarro participated. This exhibition proved that the Impressionists' theory and practice of art no longer existed as a unified tendency, although it was to become an essential basis for the modern movement in art. The young artists were torn in different directions as they tried to capture a reality which always seemed to evade their grasp. Each one on his own account sought after a mode of expression which could placate his anxiety, so different from the contemplative serenity of the generation which preceded them: Paul Cézanne sought absolute form in the Provence landscape, Seurat imprisoned light in crystal balls with the punctiliousness of a scientist, Gauguin took the path of 'synthesis', of broad, flat expanses of colour, while Van Gogh's faith and despair found expression in swirling lines of dense colour. Divisionism, pointillism, synthetism, symbolism, expressionism, Pont-Aven and the Nabis, Japanese prints and Art Nouveau — these were the generating forces of the new currents in art. Toulouse-Lautrec, the youngest of those whose artistic experience was lived in the last thirty years of the century, knew all these schools, but belonged only to himself; however, he took what he needed from these fertile cross-currents and adapted it to his own instinct and genius until it became his own.

Like all great artists, Lautrec created a personal vision, which was neither an anecdotal documentation of a particular period in a particular city nor a homage to any formula or school. At the age of seventeen he wrote to Joyant: 'I've tried to portray truth, not the ideal. This is perhaps a fault, for warts get no mercy from me, and I like to adorn them with sprightly hairs, to round them off and put a shiny tip on them.'

However, at the time when Lautrec was a boy and drawing was ceasing to be just a pleasant pastime and becoming a vital necessity, Impressionism was still the reigning force. His first paintings, *Gunner saddling his Horse* (*pl. 1*), *The Dog-Cart* (*pls 2-3*) and the others in Albi, are rather conventional student work, dating from late 1878 and early 1879. The subject-matter of horses, carriages, hunts, racing and military manoeuvres was suggested to him by his daily observation of the life around him in the aristocratic circles in which he moved, and by the horse paintings of Princeteau. From his master Henri also learned the technique of applying colours side by side with light brushstrokes, a technique related to the Impressionists' systematic decomposition of tones; it was a summary technique but was easily adaptable and enabled Lautrec to make improvisations and variations of his own. The works executed in Nice in 1880, light figures of horsewomen lifted by their grooms, elegant people driving large open carriages against a background of sea and palm-trees — show a progress in the artist's ability to indicate movement and outline, and following the example of the fashionable artists John Lewis Brown and Forain, they already denote Lautrec's tendency to emphasize gesture and silhouette at the expense of detail. The same technique of loose touches of colour is used to construct the simple relationship between the sombre tones of the background and the rubicund figure of the *Priest* (Albi, 1882), one of the few examples of Lautrec's painting whose origins may be traced to Delacroix and Courbet. But very soon the chance elements of Lautrec's first manner were replaced by a greater precision. It is true that the interplay of light and shade in *Countess A. de Toulouse-Lautrec in her Garden* (Albi) recalls the style of Berthe Morisot, but the *Portrait of a Knife-Grinder* and *Countess A. de Toulouse-Lautrec at Breakfast* (*pl. 8*) show a more personal and knowledgeable approach.

Neither the Bonnat nor the Cormon academy had succeeded in halting the development of Lautrec's personal manner, and this grew more and more marked in his drawings and paintings, especially in the portraits executed between 1885-89. The results of his academic training show themselves not so much in the allegorical works like *The Springtime of Life* (Albi), as in his attitude of mockery towards official art and literary symbolism shown, for example, in his parody of Puvis de Chavanne's *Sacred Wood* (New York, H. Pearlman coll.), exhibited at the 1884 Salon. The importance of the academies for Lautrec was that through them he could meet the young, adventurous artists, those students who were dissatisfied with Cormon and with the antiquated training of the Ecole des Beaux-Arts and were enthusiastic admirers of the innovations of the great independent artists: in the company of these young artists Lautrec's native spirit of independence was given free rein, while at the same time he absorbed the theories of Impressionism, the research made into the division of tones and colours, the cross-hatching of Pissarro and Renoir, the clarity of Raffaëlli and the drawing of Degas, whose example he openly followed in his subject-matter and his unconventional treatment.

For the Hôtel Ancelin at Villiers-sur-Morin, Lautrec painted four panels on the walls and the doors (Zurich, Bührle coll., St. Louis, Steinberg coll., Art Institute of Chicago, and the L. Pedron sale, Paris, 1926). If the style and subject-matter of these decorations call to mind Degas and Forain, the line of some of the profiles and the portrayal of the gallery crowd reveal a feeling for the grotesque and a biting irony which were unknown to those artists. But the quality of Lautrec's style during these years can best be studied in the portraits — *Van Gogh* (*pl. 12*) and *Countess A. de Toulouse-Lautrec at Malromé* (*pl. 10*) — where the background is broken up by touches of pink, blue and green, which create effects of transparent luminosity and an immediacy of colour relationships. In *The Laundress* (1889) and *Portrait of Hélène Vary* (*pl. 13*), Lautrec's line appears with greater effect through his device of giving a side view of the sitter; this was another sign of his growing awareness of his own powers and of the fact that his interest was now centred mainly on line, a line which gave firmness to the former loose patches of colour and was to lead him to results which were the antithesis of

Impressionism. In the same way, he rejected the Impressionists' love of painting in the open air, after the series of portraits executed in the garden of Père Forest between 1888-91 (*The Dancer Gabrielle*, Albi; *Justine Dieuhl*, Paris, Jeu de Paume) and eventually abandoned landscape art altogether. In fact Lautrec's main interest lay in the human figure, which he found so full of variety and movement. He was always excited by the possibility of delving into it by means of his now merciless line so as to extract the character which lay hidden behind the mask. The *Portrait of Hélène Vary*, for example, is treated in a naturalistic manner, that is to say, it is without any elements of caricature or distortion, but the same line which traced the tender profile of Hélène became biting when the artist turned to Suzanne Valadon, portrayed as *Woman Drinking* (*pls 14-15*) or the characters in *A la Mie* (*pls 26-27*), and he did not permit the actors of the Fernando Circus to escape the truth about their faces.

The Fernando Circus: Equestrian Performer (p. 18) was executed in 1888. The historical importance of this date can be seen when we consider that Seurat's *Circus* was painted in 1890. This work is significant not only because it marks the enrichment of the subject-matter of Lautrec's art with this new circus theme — a theme which was to excite Lautrec even more than Degas, and which he never abandoned, even when he was in the sanatorium, when it helped him to regain his health and liberty — but also because it marks his break with Impressionism and conventional representation in terms of perspective and shows how he has now come completely into line with Seurat, Gauguin and the Nabis. In spite of its failure to reconcile the conflicting demands of realism and pictorial vision, this picture already contains all the elements of Lautrec's personal language as it appeared in his succeeding compositions: the bold placing of the figures in the composition, with the point of vision elevated and the foreground so protruding that the figures become distorted; the famous Monsieur Loyal and the bareback rider on the foreshortened mass of the horse; the silhouettes of the motionless spectators in the background; the flat application of colour, which

Fernando Circus: Equestrian Performer, 1888. Art Institute of Chicago (Joseph Winterbotham coll.). See p. 33.

has now lost any naturalistic significance and is put on in flat areas; and finally, a taste for portraying people at a moment when they are in motion, playing or dancing, so that their gestures serve to reveal their characters.

Lautrec's vivid interest in the life of the populace increased in proportion to the growth of the dynamic forces in his painting; the more it expressed what was ever-changing and transitory, the closer it came to the taste of the public. It therefore seems quite normal that he should have devoted himself to the illustration of journals and newspapers, such as *Le Courrier Français* (where his first cartoon, *Gin Cocktail* [*pl. 9*] appeared in 1886), *Le Mirliton* (1886-7), *Le Figaro Illustré* (1893-4), *Escarmouche* (1893-4), *La Revue Blanche* (1894-5) and *Le Rire* (1894-7). For *Paris Illustré* he produced a series of cartoons which were aimed at bourgeois conformity (*The First Communion*, Toulouse,

18

Musée des Augustins: *The Omnibus Company Horse*, Paris, J. Dubourg coll., 1888); the readers did not greatly care for this kind of ' social irony ', and it brought the artist scant success. Lautrec's frequent use of the cartoon owed much to Raffaëlli, and the influence of this artist can be seen in his technique of applying colours singly, without mixing them on the palette, in light touches upon backgrounds of grey or beige, the colours of which were incorporated into the scheme of the whole composition. This method represented a further step in the direction of lightening his palette, which tended to become more and more simplified, with a range of only a few cold, pale colours, ignoring the use of either bitumen or burnt sienna; it was only later, when he encountered Japanese prints, that he added pure gold. Colour was rarely employed in such a way that it revealed the sensuality of the artist through warmth and texture. The livid tones convey instead an atmosphere of unreality.

From 1890, with the exception of the portraits of the Dinhau family (Albi, and Dinhau coll., Paris), Lautrec cared little for representing the atmospheric changes in light so beloved of the Impressionists. He preferred a cold light, which, being itself inert, did not alter the features and so enabled the painter to search into the human face in order to wrest from it its secret and accentuate its expression, unsoftened by any trace of merciful shadow. At Cormon's studio and in the years before 1890, Lautrec had met the most important artists of his time, those who had gone beyond Impressionism and were evolving ideas of their own: Degas, whose influence was so beneficent in his determination to see clearly and deeply certain aspects of life (but the vision of Degas is complete and fulfilled, whereas the restless line of Lautrec seems unable to find peace); Van Gogh, who became his friend; Emile Bernard and Louis Anquetin, the initiators of ' cloisonnisme ' (a technique using heavy outline, later carried to extremes by Gauguin); finally, still at Cormon's, Toulouse-Lautrec had his introduction to Japanese prints. Lautrec's passion for design, for undulant rhythms and vibrant echoes, first led him to revere Degas, but now urged him towards

Gauguin; his temperament, much more intense and less wide-ranging than Gauguin's, soon transformed all he learned into a style which was entirely personal.

By about 1890 his style was already completely formed. The great composition *Ball at the Moulin Rouge* (*pls 18-20*), was in fact painted in the year 1890; here the artist created a whole world of excitement and carnality, of apathy and indifference; the composition is built up on a series of asymmetrical planes placed one over the other, and the harsh glare of the lights forms an arabesque pattern of the shadow cast by the dancers on the floor, in the space enclosed by the groups of inattentive figures in the foreground. The line running through the composition seems obsessed by rhythm: it does not flow smoothly but proceeds in painful spurts, urged on by the exigencies of expressiveness. The same rhythm transforms the extraordinary mask of Nelly C. in *At the Moulin Rouge* (p. 21) into a green and yellow lamp, and gives the dark figures of La Goulue's companions (*La Goulue entering between two women*, 1892, New York, Museum of Modern Art) the flattened appearance of a Japanese screen. Lautrec returned frequently to La Goulue: her insolent beauty, carnal vulgarity and wild abandon to the dance expressed the essence of the animal vitality Lautrec asked of his models.

Lautrec's violent confrontation with reality was not dictated by his intention to caricature his subjects, for he was not so concerned to make his sitter ridiculous as to find out the truth behind the mask of youth and physical splendour which she wears: his 'stars' are already old, and the line which foreshortens their silhouettes seems to foreshorten their existence also. Each one is portrayed as she will appear in the future: La Goulue as a wild beast, the wiry agility of Jane Avril dulled into a painful rhythm, Yvette Guilbert stiff and bony, her features twisted like those of a hideous bird, May Milton and May Belfort as mature, insipid babies. Lautrec did not seek to relate his images to an 'ideal type' of womanhood, but took them as subordinate elements to a unifying form, to a line which does not flow smoothly and sensuously over the surface, as in Art Nouveau, but acts as a brake, constricting the forms and emphasizing certain features, so that the viewer is brought up short and forced to look.

In the period 1891-4 Lautrec deliberately drew closer to the Art Nouveau technique of the 'ornate in movement' which attained its maximum intensity of expression during the last decade of the century. The 'serpentine dance'

At the Moulin Rouge, 1892. Art Institute of Chicago (H. Birch Bartlett coll.). *See p. 35.*

of Loïe Fuller was a theme which inspired many sculptures and drawings (the most famous is by Bradley) because it provided an image which was not anthropomorphic but abstract, like animated ornament; this was the inspiration of *Loïe Fuller at the Folies Bergère* (*pl. 37*).

But it was the posters rather than the paintings which drew on the techniques of Art Nouveau, because their intrinsic character is that of immediate communication and 'art of the street'. The first of the non-impressionistic posters — without shadow or perspective — was the one made in 1877 by Jules Chéret for the Folies Bergère; in 1889 this artist also produced a poster for the opening of the Moulin Rouge, which is universally considered a masterpiece. But the poster made by Lautrec in 1891 for the reopening of the Moulin Rouge seemed really revolutionary: it was printed in four colours and the composition was constructed on the foreshortened perspectives of the Chinese shadows in the background, the dancing figure of La Goulue, the focal point of all eyes, and the dehumanized mask of Valentin, and contains a degree of brutality and energy which are not to be found in the posters of Chéret. In the years following 1890 therefore, with Bonnard (his poster *France-Champagne* was made in 1891) and Lautrec, the poster which until that time had been considered an inferior form of craft, became a work of art, able to fulfil not only the demands of clarity and dissemination but also the decorative requirements of Art Nouveau. In *The Garden of Paris* (1892-3), where the musical instruments in the foreground come to form a strange species of exotic flora with the distorted features of the musicians, in the figure of *Aristide Bruant at Les Ambassadeurs*, 1892, and *Aristide Bruant*, 1893 (*pls 33 and 34*) created from a few shapes of colour enclosed within flowing but precise outlines, in the decorative whimsicality of the trefoil shape on the left of the *Moulin Rouge* poster, and especially in the two-dimensional profile of Jane Avril in *Le Divan Japonais* (1892-3, *pl. 32*), it is easy to point to the extent to which concrete reality, whose characteristics were still implicit in the vigorous synthesism of Gauguin, has now been superseded. But Lautrec never reached the stage of complete dematerialization, as, for example, in the incorporeal creations of Beardsley or in the liquescent forms of Bonnard.

Lautrec could not do without reality, a human, suffering, carnal reality: it is no accident that so many of his works are devoted to the world of prostitution. His solidarity with the women who subverted even the discipline of sentiment came to him — he too an anarchist in society — not only through his need to be able to forget his appearance and to find ' the simple conversation which represents a healing silence to the spirit, a silence which is alive ' (Mac Orlan, 1934), but also through the desire, which was common to the dissipated world of Bohemian Paris to which he belonged by right, to declare himself an outsider and a rebel against bourgeois society.

As early as 1892 Lautrec had agreed naturally to the request of the *patronne* of the brothel in the Rue d' Amboise that he should decorate the drawing-room: in sixteen medallions set in rococo cornices he portrayed the heads of the brothel girls, paying homage to the bad taste employed in the decoration of the brothels where an absurd luxury corresponded to the clients' conventional idea of vice or sin, and amusing himself at the expense of those seekers after a cheap means of escape in depicting Mireille or Rolande in the languid pose of a noblewoman of the time of Louix XV. But in the numerous drawings, pastels and oils produced about this time the girls are shown in all kinds of poses, putting on their stockings or taking off a blouse, combing their hair or washing themselves, lying in bed, during the inspection, yet all without any vulgar allusion to their calling: the client — if he is present — is indicated by a top hat lying on a chair, by a shadow on a wall, or a coat hanging from a nail; his face is without importance, or rather he has no face. Lautrec gave an account — without comment and without drama — of a world which seems to have had its own paradoxical rules and dignities in his eyes.

At Rue des Moulins (pls 42-3) represents a synthesis of all these sketches and has the value of a historical composition: there is a sense of solitude in the impenetrable waiting figure of the women seen against the luxurious background of an incredible Assyrian-Babylonian décor; the scene is bathed in a warm and enveloping purple light which unifies the silhouettes of the isolated women and sets off in particularly sharp relief the only face which does not bear the marks of abandonment to a wretched availability — that of the *patronne*, who is wearing a severe-cut lilac dress. Lautrec's obsession with the human figure, always new and dynamic in his eyes, led him to explore the theatre and music-hall, the circus and the world of sport; this interest never left him and culminated in the two large panels he painted in 1895 for the sideshow at the Foire du Trône where La Goulue was displaying her declining talents. Lautrec had always been fond of decorative art and examples are to be found in all periods of his life, from his student days with Bonnat and Cormon when he produced such studio works as *The Springtime of Life*, to the decoration of the Hôtel Ancelin at Villiers-sur-Morin and the more recent decoration of the Louis XV drawing-room in the Rue d' Amboise brothel. He also designed the scenery for the first act of *The Terracotta Chariot*, a Hindu legend staged at the Théâtre de l' Oeuvre in 1894 by Lugné-Poe; in Albi there are a tapestry cartoon and a water colour for the set of *Paul et Virginie*, performed at Bordeaux in 1896. The scenery of the Théâtre de l' Oeuvre production evoked the essential atmosphere of an Indian landscape, and in its fragmented treatment which was clearly influenced by Japanese prints it must have been very similar to the two panels painted for La Goulue. The *Moorish Dance* panel (*pls 52-53*) confirms the influence of the art of Yoshiwara and Utamaro: the treatment of space ignores perspective, and the composition is built upon an interplay of slanting and horizontal lines, juxtaposed figures and a colour scheme whose subdued tones are without any descriptive function and purely decorative; while the dry, shaven features of Fénéon and his Oriental inscrutability set the seal on the Japanese quality of this work. In *Cha-U-Kao* (1895, *pl. 55*) Lautrec uses broad strokes of yellow, blue, red and white and sharp, rapid lines, to give the picture depth and an extraordinary vivacity. He portrays this strange female clown as natural in the midst of her artificiality, pathetic in her boastfulness and tired in her strength: 'this is perhaps the highest expression of the artist's ideal' (L. Venturi, 1950, p. 181). It was the happiest and most fertile period of Lautrec's creativity.

With the illustrative technique which he reserved for lithography rather than painting, Lautrec executed bills for two English singers, May Milton and May Belfort (*pl. 54*); in a series of drawings he captured the amazing agility of a Negro acrobat, *Chocolat Dancing at Achille's Bar* (1896, *pl. 60*); and portrayed *Oscar Wilde* (1895, Beverley Hills, California, Lester coll.) as an obese night bird against the foggy background of the Thames, all his exhausted sensuality expressed in the drooping lines round his mouth. He made many portraits of his friends: *Dr Gabriel Tapié de Céleyran* (1894, *pl. 45*) against a glowing red carpet; the actress *Berthe Body* (1897, *pl. 69*); *Cipa Godebski* (1896, Paris, Niarchos coll.), a massive-featured Pole; the corpulent *Maxime Dethomas* (1896, *pl. 62*); and the friends who gathered around the *Revue blanche*, the most progressive of the journals devoted to art, literature and politics — Paul Leclerq, Tristan Bernard, Jules Renard, Romain Coolus, Felix Fénéon, the Natansons — the friends who had joined the circle of the studio companions, Anquetin, Grenier and Gauzi, and of the younger painters, Vuillard, Vallotton and Bonnard. Lautrec's friendship with Tristan Bernard, the manager of the Vélodrome Buffalo, gave him entry to the world of sport, whose elements of competitiveness and movement corresponded to his own conception of beauty; he produced posters for the bicycle manufacturers and made portraits of athletes, and of his friend, *Bernard at the Vélodrome Buffalo* (1895, New York, Isles coll.).

Although Lautrec's sparkling vitality gradually gave way to a growing irritability which changed his vivacious expression into the dull gaze of the alcoholic and his speech into unintelligible outbursts, he continued to produce, and exerted an extraordinary willpower in seeking for new forms, so as to avoid repeating himself. In the years around and immediately following 1897 he often returned to the themes and techniques of his youth, but now he brought greater knowledge and maturity to bear on them: *Madame Poupoule Dressing* (1894, Albi), with fragmented tones, changing as they fall on her hair, her clothes and even the background to the picture; *Portrait of Paul Leclerq* (1897, *pls 66-67*), where the subtle, colloquial interpretation is oblivious of the cruel distortions of earlier years; and even his illustrations of Jules Renard's *Histoires Naturelles* (published by Fleury in 1899), with figures of animals such as he had liked to paint in his youth, all give proof of this return to the past.

In lithography also, although he now spent much less time on this medium, he experimented with a new technique, which, being less concentrated, enabled him to economize his means in order to attain greater precision and refinement: *The Passenger in Cabin 54* (1896, *pl. 63*), executed from memory, was composed in six colours on a pattern of crossing lines which become less tense in the receding seascape, and the intense, mysterious figure of the woman is the first of the tender female portraits which Lautrec painted towards the end of his life. Among these are his finest portrait of Croquesi-Margouin (*pls 76-77*), the girl with the pointed profile, and the last to arouse the love of the artist, who always felt starved of affection; and *English Dancer at 'The Star', Le Havre* (1899, *pls 71 and 72*), a symphony in blue, green and violet. In both these works, but in the latter especially, Lautrec aspired to a 'compendiary' technique in the manner of Cézanne, a return to areas of light and shade, with vibrations of colour suggesting luminous effects. A similar treatment occurs in the circus drawings executed in the sanatorium at Neuilly, with greater emphasis on plasticity. These drawings too represent a return to the theme of Lautrec's youth: the bodies of Footit and Chocolat, the horsewoman, the acrobats, the bear Caviar, seem to have grown in size and weight and to have hardened within their bright outlines in a light which holds them suspended in empty space.

After this short, happy period in his artistic production, Lautrec was never to recover his old fire; even his colour became leaden and his images of a flaccid and displeasing monumentality (*Portrait of Maurice Joyant*, 1900, *pl. 75*; *Messalina*, 1901, Art Institute of Chicago). The technical evolution, which he attempted but probably did not bring to fruition, foundered in the awkward *Examination at the Faculty of Medicine* (1901, *pls 78-79*), where his usual sharp outline is replaced by heavy masses of colour, anticipating the violent juxtapositions of Rouault.

It is difficult to confine Lautrec to any historical period: he belonged to no school, and, although he was aware of contemporary trends, he managed to avoid any kind of label. However, he showed his sympathy for the innovators of art forms through the few official acts of his life: with Degas, Raffaëlli, Renoir and others, he subscribed to the purchase of Manet's *Olympia*, which they presented to the Louvre; and he showed his work at the exhibitions of Les Vingt and at the Salon des Indépendants, which were important events for all those artists who worked outside the academic tradition. Just as he had had no masters, so he had no pupils; he certainly could not ignore the fact that he influenced the development of such younger artists as Bonnard, Vuillard and Vallotton, but his attitude towards them was·always that of equal to equal. However, as we look back over a greater distance in time, we see how great was his importance as an influence on the artists who succeeded him — and first and foremost on Pablo Picasso. As a painter, Lautrec's style was rather summary and unworked, and his best paintings were produced during the ten years 1888-98; the ease with which he assimilated the techniques of other artists and manipulated them to his own ends was due to his desire to work quickly, hurrying to create the painting immediately after the sketch or gesture which had suggested it to him. This often made the paintings seem unfinished, so that it is necessary to select them carefully.

In the graphic field, to which a large part of his production was devoted, he was undoubtedly an artist of the first rank. Many of his drawings were made with a view to lithographic reproduction, and here he was an outstanding innovator. Like Munch, Gauguin and Seurat, he mainly sought after linear effects, and lithography offered unlimited scope for his originality. With its spatial illusions and areas of brilliant colour, lithography was made to rival oil painting, in which indeed Lautrec recognized no superiority. The driving force of Lautrec's line represents the true quality of his art — it is an imperious line which tears apart man and beast with equal fury, then recreates and unifies them in an endless arabesque. In Lautrec's drawings there is all the strangeness, the fantastic energy, the passion and brutality which mark all great graphic artists from Bosch to Klee, making something animal out of the human and something human of the animal, studying reality only to violate it.

Toulouse-Lautrec is a modern artist, and today we are more able than our grandparents to understand him. Our electrically-lit surroundings form an even less natural kind of 'habitat' than that of seventy years ago; our belief that art should not be for the privileged few makes us value prints as a less costly form of art which can be accessible to everyone; we think that art can be produced out of everyday objects, in the same way as Lautrec — who did not distinguish between 'pure art' and 'commercial art' — made works of art from theatre programmes, invitation cards or menus; then too, posters, the 'art of the streets', form an intrinsic element of our landscape and we are attracted to their bold style and conditioned by their message; lastly, Lautrec's arbitrary compositions, with the foreground brought up close to the viewer and with space suddenly receding into the distance as beams of light fall on the vacant faces of the actors in his human comedy, belong to the world of still photography and the cinema. The 'moral surgery' which is not the least quality of his art (Ragghianti, 1944) makes Toulouse-Lautrec a visionary precursor of the twentieth century.

Lautrec and the Critics

' Lautrec was fated for the lunatic asylum. He was committed yesterday, and now the mask has fallen and madness will officially sign the pictures, drawings and posters where before it was anonymous ' (A. Hepp, *Le Journal*, 26 March 1899). ' We are wrong to pity Lautrec, we must envy him ... the only place where happiness can be found is always the cell of an asylum ' (E. Lepelletier, *Echo de Paris,* 20 March 1899). ' A few days ago we lost an artist who had acquired celebrity of an ugly kind ... Toulouse-Lautrec, a bizarre and deformed being, who saw everything through his own physiological wretchedness .... He died miserably, ruined in body and spirit, in an asylum, a prey to attacks of dementia. A sad end to a sad life ' (Jumelles, *Lyon Républicain*, 15 September 1901). ' Just as there are enthusiastic lovers of the bullfight, executions and other sordid spectacles, so there are admirers of Toulouse-Lautrec. It is a good thing for humanity. that there are few artists of this kind ' (J. Rocques, *Le Courrier Français*, 15 September 1901).

These are extracts from some of the articles which appeared in the press at the time of Lautrec's stay in the asylum and his death. There is no need to stress their vindictiveness, for it is obvious enough — indeed, one might think that those who indulged in this vituperation had forgotten even that ordinary pity generally reserved for those who through sickness or death abandon the scene of life. The strangeness of the appearance and life of Lautrec, together with the taste of the public, which was corrupted by an academic tradition and a love of naturalistic anecdote, and the universal custom of indulging in violent polemics, represented for Lautrec's contemporaries a barrier against balanced criticism. Even in the best cases, that is, when the critic managed to avoid speaking of his talent as that of an unfortunate cripple who always sought the sordid things in life, he was referred to as a pleasing illustrator or as an unhappy man seeking for escape, a

Bohemian gnome or a bored aristocrat. In fact Lautrec was a prisoner of his own persona, and while he was alive there were few who took the trouble to recognize his qualities as an artist. It was only the most sensitive critics who appreciated him: Tristan Bernard (*La Revue Blanche*, 1895), Gustave Geffroy (*La Vie Artistique*, 1900, and *Gazette des Beaux Arts*), Roger Marx (*La Revue Universelle*, 1901) and Arsène Alexandre (*Le Figaro*, 1899). His detractors sinned through injustice, incomprehension or sheer vindictiveness; and his admirers let themselves be swayed by their affection for him as a man and a friend, their respect for his courage and human sympathy. They too, though for opposite motives, forgot the artist.

However, the Lautrec bibliography is based on the articles which appeared in the press and on memoirs, letters and notes by his friends and relatives: G. Coquiot (1913 and 1920), P. Leclerq (1921), P. Mac Orlan (1934), A. Astre (1938), Th. Natanson (1938 and 1952), F. Jourdain (1950, 1951, 1954), F. Gauzi (1954) and M. Tapié de Céleyran (1953); but the basic study is that by Lautrec's lifelong friend Maurice Joyant (Paris, 1926-7, 2 vols.). The biography is pervaded by a brotherly affection and is a well-documented, clear account of the artist's life and works.

The Musée Toulouse-Lautrec in Albi was opened on 30 July 1922 in the presence of Léon Bérard, Minister of Education, and this official recognition was a public acknowledgment of Lautrec's genius. Since then there have been frequent exhibitions of Lautrec's work in Europe and the United States: the most important include the exhibition of graphic works held at the Bibliothèque Nationale (catalogue by J. Adhémar), the exhibition of paintings held at the Orangerie, Paris (catalogue with preface by M. Florisoone and introduction by M. G. Dortu) on the fiftieth anniversary of the painter's death, and the exhibitions held at the Petit Palais, Paris, and at Albi to mark the centenary of his birth (catalogue prefaced by J. Bouchot-Daupique).

In recent years many works have been written on the subject of Lautrec, but this literature is often obscure or contradictory. However, mention should be made of some studies which throw light on particular aspects of Lautrec's style: the article by H. Focillon (in *Gazette des Beaux Arts*, 1931), R. Pallucchini *Gli Impressionisti alla XXIV Biennale*, catalogue (1948), L. Venturi (in the volume, *Da Manet a Lautrec*, 1950), G. Veronesi (*Emporium*, 1951), C. L. Ragghianti (*Sele-Arte*, 1952), N. Ponente (in *Encyclopaedia of World Art*, XIV, 1966), A. Chastel (Collins-UNESCO, 1966).

For works containing large numbers of reproductions the reader should consult: F. Jourdain and J. Adhémar (Paris 1952), J. Lassaigne (Geneva, 1953), D. Cooper (New York 1952 and Paris 1955), and especially Ph. Huisman and M. G. Dortu (*Lautrec par Lautrec*, Paris 1964), and finally H. Keller (Cologne 1968; ed. Dumont) and the recent monograph by F. Novotny (London 1969).

For the graphic works reference must be made to the two volumes by L. Delteil, *Le peintre-graveur illustré*. Mention must also be made of at least J. Bouchot-Saupique (*Les Arts Plastiques*, VII, 1947), R. Huyghe (*Le Dessin Français au XIX siècle*, Lausanne, 1948) and F. Novotny (*The Burlington Magazine*, June 1949).

To the catalogues already mentioned must be added those of the Musée Toulouse-Lautrec, Albi, edited by E. Julien (1952) and the recent *60 Oeuvres inconnues de Toulouse-Lautrec* (preface by J. Devoisins) which contains the drawings, mainly early works, which were exhibited from June to September 1969 in Albi.

Notes on the Plates

1 Gunner saddling his Horse, 1879. Canvas, 0.50×0.37 m. Albi, Musée Toulouse-Lautrec.

2-3 The Dog-Cart, 1880. Panel, 0.27×0.35 m. Albi, Musée Toulouse-Lautrec.

4 The Falconer, 1881. Panel, 0.23×0.14 m. Albi, Musée Toulouse-Lautrec. Painted at Céleyran or Le Bosc. The subject is the artist's father, Count Alphonse de Toulouse-Lautrec, shown setting off on a hawking expedition with one of his falcons: he wears a picturesque Circassian costume and is seated on an Arab horse. Although the execution is immature, the picture conveys the ironic regard felt by Lautrec for this outdated, provincial society.

5 A Priest, 1881. Canvas, 0.40×0.32 m. Albi, Musée Toulouse-Lautrec.

6 Nude Study: Woman seated on a Divan, 1882. 0.55×0.46 m. Albi, Musée Toulouse-Lautrec. The treatment is delicate, and the grey tones mingle with the pink of the divan to create a vibrant light.

7 Head of a Child: Severino Rossi, 1883. Charcoal, 0.62×0.47 m. Albi, Muséee Toulouse-Lautrec.

8 Countess A. de Toulouse-Lautrec at Breakfast, 1883. Canvas, 0.93×0.81 m. Albi, Musée Toulouse-Lautrec. Between 1880 and 1887 Lautrec made three charcoal drawings and three oils of his mother. This is the second of the three paintings and shows the influence of Manet, not only by its quiet tone, but because the artist does not allow the sitter to appear separate from her surroundings but makes her one with the table and the window, open to the dazzling light.

9 Gin Cocktail, 1886. Charcoal, 0.47×0.62 m. Albi, Musée Toulouse-Lautrec. This is a first study for the drawing which appeared in *Le Courrier Français* on 25 September 1886.

10 Countess A. de Toulouse-Lautrec at Malromé, 1887. Canvas, 0.59×0.54 m. Albi, Musée Toulouse-Lautrec. This is the third portrait of Lautrec's mother, and is taken from an academic charcoal drawing (1885, Albi). However, the painting recalls the manner of Manet and Pissarro: like the Impressionists, Lautrec wished to portray his sitters in their surroundings, yet it is clear that his interest was already turning towards the human presence which acquires physical prominence and psychological depth by being placed in a position firmly in the foreground, while the background and surrounding area became less important as Lautrec's feeling for objects and landscape grew colder.

11   The Last Farewell, 1886. Charcoal, 0.63 × 0.44 m. Albi, Musée Toulouse-Lautrec. Study from life for a drawing which appeared in *Le Mirliton* in March 1887 to illustrate one of Bruant's songs.

12   Portrait of Van Gogh, 1887. Pastel on cardboard, 0.45 × 0.54 m. Amsterdam, Stedelijk Museum. This portrait is exceptional because it is executed in pastel, a medium rarely used by Lautrec, and because in his choice of colours and technique of rapid brush-strokes he appears to be influenced by the style of Van Gogh himself.

13   Portrait of Hélène Vary, 1888. Cardboard, 0.34 × 0.19 m. Albi, Musée Toulouse-Lautrec. Here the artist probably used a photograph as his starting point. His colours are restrained, orchestrated on variations of blue, and again the brushstrokes recall the manner of Van Gogh. The same figure, now with hands resting on her lap, can be seen in a painting in the Bremen Kunsthalle.

Fernando Circus: Equestrian Performer, 1888. Canvas, 0.98 × 1.61 m. Illustration p. 18. Art Institute of Chicago (Joseph Winterbotham coll). Probably completed during the year 1888. Exhibited in the foyer of the Moulin Rouge in October 1889, where it was seen by Seurat, who certainly remembered it when he painted his *Circus* in 1890-1. The daring composition was inspired by Degas, but here Lautrec breaks with naturalistic representation and obtains a highly stylized image through his contemplation of a dynamic event. The jerky, broken outlines of the previous works have now been replaced by an essential linearity, with agile forms and decisive rhythms. The colour dynamics are still present in the intersecting lines, but the treatment is now very simplified as compared with earlier works. It was this new simplification which paved the way for Lautrec's lithographic art, and this painting is its most significant forerunner.

14-15   Woman Drinking, 1889. Cardboard, 0.55 × 0.46 m. Harvard University, Fogg Art Museum. The subject is Marie Clémentine Valade (1867-1938), the mother of Maurice Utrillo, who painted under the name Suzanne Valadon. This portrait was painted shortly before the bitter quarrel which separated the two artists. It was based on several preliminary drawings, one of which (Albi) later appeared in *Le Courrier Français* on 21 April 1890. Two previous portraits of Suzanne Valadon were painted by Lautrec, one in the Carlsberg Museum, Copenhagen (1885), the other in the Museo de Bellas Artes, Buenos Aires (1886).

16-17   Ball at the Moulin de la Galette, 1889. Canvas, 0.88 × 100 m. Art Institute of Chicago. Exhibited at the Salon des Indépendants in March 1889; the preparatory drawing was reproduced in *Le Courrier Français* on 10 May 1889. This is Lautrec's second large composition, and compared with *Fernando Circus: Equestrian Performer* (p. 18) it shows considerable progress, since it has greater spatial coherence and is without the caricatural accentuation of the features which marred the earlier work. The man seen on the left in a felt hat is the painter Joseph Albert, the first owner of this painting.

18-20   Ball at the Moulin Rouge, 1890. Canvas, 1.15×1.50 m. Philadelphia, H. P. McIlhenny coll. This is Lautrec's third large composition. It was painted only one year after *Ball at the Moulin de la Galette*, and yet it is a much more complex work, composed on three planes. It was exhibited in 1890 in the foyer of the Moulin Rouge, a music hall which had opened the year before on the Boulevard de Clichy in Montmartre, and was frequented by an elegant, vivacious public. Several famous people and friends of the artist can be recognized: the four men in the centre between La Goulue and the woman in red are Verney, Guibert, Sescau and Gauzi, and the woman wearing a black cloak is Jane Avril. In the years 1890-6 Lautrec did at least thirty paintings inspired by the Moulin Rouge.

21   Mlle Dihau playing the Piano, 1890. Cardboard, 0.68×0.48 m. Albi, Musée Toulouse-Lautrec. Close ties of friendship linked Lautrec with the Dihau family, Désiré, Henri and their sister Marie, all musicians. The theme of a woman seated at the piano was taken up again in such works as *Mme Pascal* (1895, Albi) and *Misia Natanson* (1897, New York, Tannhauser coll.): as we are told by Joyant, this subject interested Lautrec greatly, because he found the hands more exciting than the face and boasted that he was able to make ' portraits of hands '.

22   Le Nouveau Cirque, 1891. Cardboard, 1.19×0.87 m. Philadelphia Museum of Art. This is certainly the study for a poster, which was not executed. The broad composition and loose perspective are typical of the drawings which Lautrec intended to transfer later onto lithographic stone.

23   La Goulue at the Moulin Rouge, 1891. Poster (L.D. 339; J.A.I), 1.25×1.22 m. Paris, Cabinet des Estampes. Exhibited at the Salon des Indépendants in 1892. This is the first of Lautrec's posters; it was published by Lévy in four colours (yellow, red, blue, black) and today is considered a classic of lithographic art. The emphasized foreground, the surface colour tension which includes the areas occupied by the figures, the strengthening of tone and line so that the more the figures lose proportion the more they gain in immediacy, all these factors perfectly fulfil the requirements of an art devoted to the everyday aspects of life. The perspective is constructed on three planes and this forces the eye to undergo a series of ' shocks ': as it lights on La Goulue, the only flesh-and-blood figure, who is made dynamic and corporeal by the evocative and summary line on the insubstantial figure of Valentin and on the silhouettes of the spectators seen in negative against the background line. Note how the expressionistic significance of the shape of Valentin, arrested and foreshortened in the swirling movement of the dance, is balanced and given emphasis by the unexpected yellow form glowing on the left: this naturalistic detail of the lamplight is used to create an entirely unreal image.

The preparatory sketch for this poster, in charcoal with touches of colour, is now in Albi. The numbering of Lautrec's graphic work relates to the catalogues of Loys Delteil (1920 L.D.) and Jean Adhémar (1965, J.A.).

24-25 A Corner of the Moulin de la Galette, 1891. Canvas, 1.50×0.89 m. Washington, National Gallery of Art. Exhibited at Goupil's in February 1891 and at the Salon des Indépendants in autumn of that year. It is not certain that the subject is in fact the Moulin de la Galette, but the work is probably based on an episode in the life of the music halls.

26-27 A la Mie, 1891. Cardboard, 0.53×0.68. Boston, Museum of Art. Exhibited at the Salon des Indépendants in 1892. The work is derived from a photograph taken by Paul Sescau of the amateur painter Maurice Guibert and a young model. The painting is clearly inspired by Degas' *L'Absinthe*, but Lautrec is more determined than Degas to show his models as masks of moral and physical degradation, taking no heed of their charm and youth.

28 The Moulin Rouge: the start of the quadrille, 1892. Gouache on cardboard, 0.80×0.61 m. Washington, National Gallery of Art (C. Dale Loan coll.). Another episode in the life of the music hall: the public withdraws to the tables of the *promenoir*, leaving the floor to the dancers of the ' naturalist quadrille '. This dance was a return to the cancan which had been fashionable between 1850 and 1870, and as performed by La Goulue and Valentin-le-Désossé it had a great success.

At the Moulin Rouge, 1892. Illustration p. 21. Canvas, 1.23×1.40 m. Art Institute of Chicago (H. Birch Bartlett coll.). Life as a collective and changing phenomenon and experience of life as a mirror of society continued to be Lautrec's only focus of interest, the only spectacle which could appease his curiosity. This time, the artist's attention turned to the public of the *promenoir*: seated at a table are the critic Edouard Dujardin (with a fair beard), the Spanish dancer La Macarona, and the photographer Sescau and Guibert, next to a woman seen from behind. In the background La Goulue attends to her hair in front of a mirror, while the small figure of Lautrec passes in front of his tall cousin, Dr Tapié de Céleyran; in the foreground is the oriental mask of Nelly C., added to the painting on a strip of canvas 15 cm. long which Lautrec sewed to the back of the canvas himself. The whole composition is contained within two diagonal lines: the balustrade and the axes of the floor, which form a V-shape, forcing the eye to remain fixed on the single focal point at the centre where the figures in the foreground rise to a gigantic height. The other planes follow in a accelerated, flowing rhythm, each one sharply individualized.

29 Study for the head of Mr Warner, 1892. Cardboard, 0.57×0.45 m. Albi, Musée Toulouse-Lautrec. Study for the colour lithograph, *The Englishman at the Moulin Rouge* (L.D. 12).

30 Reine de Joie, 1892. Poster (L.D. 342; J.A. 5) 1.30×0.89 m. Paris, Cabinet des Estampes. Printed by E. Ancourt as a book cover for the novel of that title by the Polish write Victor Joze (Dobsky). It was printed in four colours: black, red, green and yellow.

31 Jane Avril dancing, 1892. Cardboard, 0.85×0.45 m. Paris, Jeu de Paume. Attracted by the 'pallid, highly-strung, suffering' figure of Jane Avril, Lautrec portrayed her many times in the course of two years: dancing, entering the Moulin Rouge, leaving, putting on her gloves, in back and front view. (Albi, Courtauld Institute, London, American collections).

32 Le Divan Japonais, 1892-3. Poster (L.D. 341, J.A. 11). 0.80×0.60 m. Paris, Cabinet des Estampes. Printed by E. Ancourt in four colours: yellow, green, red and black. It was made to advertise a new music hall, Le Divan Japonais, which opened in the spring of 1893. Jane Avril is shown in the centre, on the right the music critic Dujardin, and in the background Yvette Guilbert is recognizable by her long black gloves. The organization of space is dependent on the complicated outline of the figure of Jane, with a series of protrusions and recessions: it is the triumph of the *fin-de-siècle* woman, whose elegance lay in the silhouette, comprised by an austere coat and elaborate hat.

33 Aristide Bruant at Les Ambassadeurs, 1892. Poster (L.D. 345; J.A. 6) 1.50×1.00 m. Paris, Cabinet des Estampes. Printed by E. Ancourt in six colours: yellow, mauve, blue, red, dark green and black. This is the poster which Bruant himself insisted that the management should accept.

34 Aristide Bruant, 1893. Poster (L.D. 348, J.A. 15). 1.27×0.92 m. Paris, Cabinet des Estampes. In spite of the two-dimensional treatment of space and the lack of psychological characterization, the human presence of Bruant is created out of his costume, which spreads out in waves, swells and expands, to produce a sensation of violent energy. In 1894 Lautrec made a third poster for his friend Bruant (L.D. 349), a full-length back view.

35 Caudieux, 1893. Poster (L.D. 348, J.A. 13). 1.30×0.95 m. Paris, Cabinet des Estampes. Printed by Choix in four colours: yellow, red, black and green, for the comic actor Caudieux who performed at the Petit Casino.

36 Papa Chrysanthème, 1893. Cardboard, 0.61×0.80 m. Albi, Musée Toulouse-Lautrec. For this Japanese fantasy, performed at the Nouveau Cirque in November 1892, the arena was transformed into a pond covered in lilies, lotus flowers and water plants, around which the dancers moved. Lautrec made another drawing in oils on this subject, which is also in Albi.

37 Loïe Fuller at the Folies Bergère, 1893. Cardboard, 0.63×0.45 m. Albi, Musée Toulouse-Lautrec. Study for the colour lithograph produced in the same year (L.D. 39). Loïe Fuller was an American dancer who aroused the enthusiasm of the Parisians when she appeared enveloped in veils to perform a dance known as *La Serpentine.* As she danced, the spotlight transformed her into an enormous, many-coloured ornament, a kind of floral symbol, an emblem of Art Nouveau, in which even the human figure was subjected to a process of stylization and decorative abstraction.

38 Lady and Gentleman with a Dog, 1893. Canvas, 0.48×0.60 m. Albi, Musée Toulouse-Lautrec. He studied these two owners of a brothel without pity until — by means of a graphic line which superseded colour — he obtained this striking portrait.

39 Woman at a Window, 1893. Cardboard, 0.57×0.47 m. Albi, Musée Toulouse-Lautrec.

40 Monsieur Delaporte at the Jardin de Paris, 1893. Cardboard, 0.70×0.60 m. Copenhagen, Ny Carlsberg Glyptotek. As always, only the person who is the subject of the portrait is really in focus. Among the background figures one can recognize a back view of Jane Avril, wearing an elaborate black hat.

41 Yvette Guilbert, 1894. Watercolour on paper, 0.48×0.38 m. Albi, Musée Toulouse-Lautrec. Study for the sixteenth plate of the album dedicated to Yvette (L.D. 95).

42-43 At Rue des Moulins, 1894. Canvas, 1.115×1.327 m. Albi, Musée Toulouse-Lautrec. This is the last of the series of brothel studies made between 1890 and 1894. It was preceded by a pastel study, also in Albi.

44 Yvette Guilbert, 1894. Watercolour on paper, 1.86×0.93 m. Albi, Musée Toulouse-Lautrec. This is the sketch for the poster which so offended Yvette by its brutality that she rejected it. ' You little monster, you've produced a real horror ' she is said to have exclaimed to Lautrec.

45 Dr Gabriel Tapié de Céleyran, 1894. Canvas, 1.10×0.56 m. Albi, Musée Toulouse-Lautrec.

46 The Brothel Cleaner, 1894. Cardboard, 0.57×0.46 m. Albi, Musée Toulouse-Lautrec.

47 Woman putting on her Stocking, 1894. Cardboard, 0.61×0.44 m. Albi, Musée Toulouse-Lautrec. Study for a painting with the same title (Paris, Jeu de Paume).

48 Medical Inspection at Rue des Moulins, 1894. Cardboard, 0.83×0.61 m. Washington, National Gallery. The girls file sadly past the doctor, in an orderly line. This is one of the most fearsome of the brothel works.

49 Misia Natanson, 1895. Charcoal with colour on paper, 1.50× ×1.05 m. Albi, Musée Toulouse-Lautrec. Study for the poster for *La Revue blanche.*

50-51 La Goulue's Booth: The Quadrille, 1895. Canvas, 2.98×3.10 m. Paris, Jeu de Paume. La Goulue, now fat and in decline, asked Lautrec to paint large decorative panels for the entrance to the fairground booth which she set up at the Foire du Trône. On the left side, he depicted the dancer's past glories, on the right the ' Moorish dance ' she performed at the fair.

52-53 La Goulue's Booth: Moorish Dance, 1895. Canvas, 2.98× 3.10 m. Paris, Jeu de Paume. Many of the famous are portrayed here: Sescau, at the piano, then Maurice Guilbert, the writer Félix Fénéon, Dr Tapié de Céleyran and finally Oscar Wilde, whose back view is unmistakable.

54 May Belfort, 1895. Poster (L.D. 354, J.A. 116). Paris, Cabinet des Estampes. Lautrec has portrayed the singer as she appeared during the performance which brought her success at Les Décadents, where she sang, dressed as a little girl holding a black kitten in her arms, ' Daddy Wouldn't Buy Me a Bow-wow '.

55 The Female Clown Cha-U-Kao, 1895. Cardboard, 0.64×0.49 m. Paris, Jeu de Paume. This female clown appeared at Le Nouveau Cirque and the Moulin Rouge and Lautrec portrayed her in a full-length portrait (O. Reinhardt coll., Winterthur), a half-length portrait (Powell Jones coll., Gates Mills, Ohio) and a splendid lithograph for *Elles,* as well as in this work which is in the Jeu de Paume.

56 La Goulue and Valentin le Désossé, 1895. Ink, 0.22×0.36 m. Albi, Musée Toulouse-Lautrec. Preparatory study for the decoration of La Goulue's booth at the Foire du Trône.

57 Marcelle Lender, 1895-6. Lithograph. Paris, Cabinet des Estampes. The face is that of the dancer portrayed in the large painting *Marcelle Lender dancing the Bolero at Chilpéric* (New York, J.H. Whitney coll.), one of Lautrec's most important and successful paintings. From this painting he made many versions of details and some lithographs.

58 Ambroise Thomas at a Rehearsal of 'Francesca da Rimini', 1896. Blue pencil and charcoal. 0.79×0.61 m. Albi, Musée Toulouse-Lautrec. One of the drawings made for *Le Rire*, a journal edited by Lautrec's friend Arsène Alexandre. The hat in the foreground belongs to Misia Natanson.

59 Cha-U-Kao's Entrance at the Moulin Rouge, 1896. Blue and black pencil, 0.87×0.63 m. Albi, Musée Toulouse-Lautrec. For *Le Rire*. Shrove Tuesday, 1896: Cha-U-Kao enters on the back of a mule escorted by a bodyguard. Lautrec and Tapié de Céleyran are among the bystanders (see also pl. 55).

60 Chocolat Dancing at Achille's Bar, 1896. Blue and black pencil, 0.65×0.50 m. Albi, Musée Toulouse-Lautrec. This drawing appeared in *Le Rire* on 28 March 1896.

61 The Wings at the Folies Bergère, 1896. Ink and blue pencil, 0.65×0.50 m. Albi, Musée Toulouse-Lautrec. This drawing appeared in *Le Rire* on 13 June 1896. Mrs Lona Barrison was a famous English equestrian performer and is shown with her manager and husband.

62 Maxime Dethomas at the Opera, 1896. Cardboard, 0.68×0.54 m. Washington, National Gallery of Art (C. Dale coll.).

63 The Passenger in Cabin 54, 1896. Poster (L.D. 366, J.A. 188). Paris, Cabinet des Estampes. This is the portrait of the unknown, beautiful woman who occupied Cabin 54 of the *S.S. Chili*. Lautrec was so impressed by her charms that he prolonged his journey to Dakar, but refused to meet her (he was affected by such attacks of shyness at times). This large lithograph was made from memory with the aid of a photograph.

64 La Vache Enragée, 1896. Poster (L.D. 364, J.A. 197). 0.83×0.60 m. Paris, Cabinet des Estampes. Printed by Choix in four colours (yellow, red, green and blue) for the magazine *La Vache enragée*.

65 Seated Woman, 1896. Cardboard, 0.67×0.54 m. Paris, Jeu de Paume.

66-67 Portrait of Paul Leclerq, 1897. Cardboard, 0.54×0.64 m. Paris, Jeu de Paume.

68 Woman Combing her Hair, 1896. Cardboard, 0.43×0.29 m. Paris, Jeu de Paume.

69 Portrait of Berthe Body, 1897. Cardboard, 0.70×0.60 m. Albi, Musée Toulouse-Lautrec. Berthe Body was a Belgian actress who performed at the Théâtre de l'Oeuvre, which was the centre of symbolist drama. Lautrec made lithographs and programme designs for this theatre.

70 Jane Avril, 1899. Poster (L.D. 367, J.A. 323). 0.56×0.36 m. Paris, Cabinet des Estampes. Printed by H. Stern in four colours, blue, yellow, red and black. Again the characteristic feature is the clinging, sinuous coat worn by Jane, the heroine and symbol of Art Nouveau.

71 The English Dancer at 'Le Star', Le Havre, 1899. Sanguine and gesso on grey-blue paper. 0.62×0.47 m. Albi, Musée Toulouse-Lautrec. Sketch for pl. 72.

72 The English Dancer at 'Le Star', Le Havre, 1899. Panel, 0.41×0.32 m. Albi, Musée Toulouse-Lautrec. This is the portrait of an unassuming actress, Miss Dolly, who performed at 'Le Star', Le Havre, where Lautrec saw her when he was about to embark on the *Chili*. He immediately telegraphed Joyant to ask for his painting materials.

73 At 'Le Rat-Mort', 1899-1900. Oil on canvas, 0.55×0.46 m. London, Courtauld Institute. This painting is typical of Lautrec's last period, where the line is less incisive and there is greater emphasis on effects of light. Here light travels from the head-covering to shine upon the hair, darken over the deep-set eyes and give prominence to the sneering mouth of Lucy Jourdan.

74 Cocyte in 'La Belle Hélène', 1900. Watercolour, 0.40×0.29 m. Albi, Musée Toulouse-Lautrec. This work is very typical of Lautrec's last period. It was inspired by a clumsy performance of this opera, staged with ostentatious luxury at Bordeaux.

75 Maurice Joyant, 1900. Panel, 1.16×0.81 m. Albi, Musée Toulouse-Lautrec.

76-77 Portrait of Mlle Croquesi-Margouin, 1900. Panel, 0.61×0.49 m. Albi, Musée Toulouse-Lautrec. Lautrec's last months were sweetened by the friendship of an eighteen-year-old girl, Louise Blouet. The nickname he gave her comes from *Croques-y* (sketch away!) and *margouin*, which in Parisian slang means 'mannequin', the girl's profession. Lautrec painted two other portraits of her in oils and many drawings.

78-79 Examination at the Faculty of Medicine, 1901. Canvas, 0.65×0.81 m. Albi, Musée Toulouse-Lautrec. This is the last finished painting by Lautrec. On the left, Gabriel Tapié de Céleyran (seen from the back) discusses his doctorate thesis with Professors Wurtz and Fourier.

1

29

AMBASSADEURS...

aristide BRUANT dans son cabaret

Hautrec

33

Caudieux

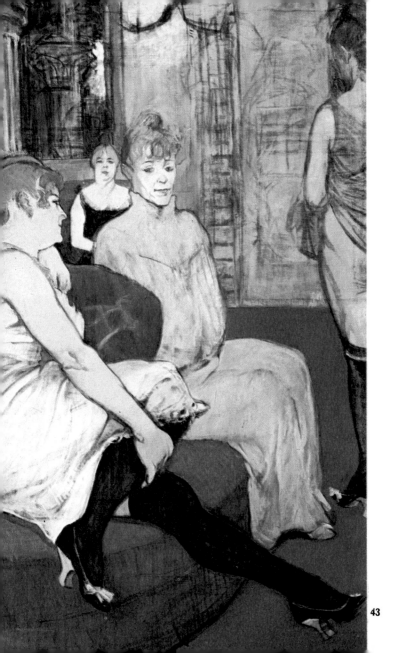

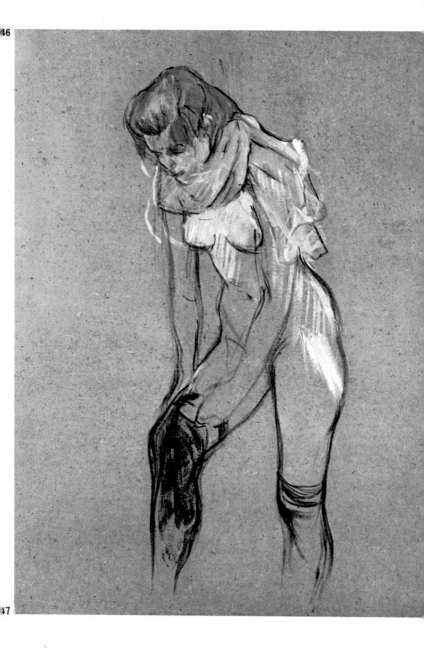

51

May Belfort

JANE
Avril

H.Stern, Paris.

1899

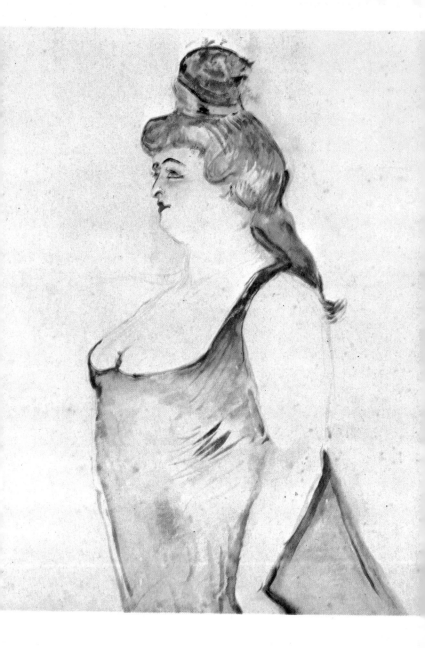